SHADY PEOPLE

A Rhyming
Children's Book
About Body Safety

Written By Jeff Davenport
Illustrated By Scott Elkins

WestBow Press books may be ordered through booksellers or by contacting:

WestBow Press
A Division of Thomas Nelson & Zondervan
1663 Liberty Drive
Bloomington, IN 47403
www.westbowpress.com
1 (866) 928-1240

Because of the dynamic nature of the Internet, any web addresses or links contained in
this book may have changed since publication and may no longer be valid. The views
expressed in this work are solely those of the author and do not necessarily reflect the
views of the publisher, and the publisher hereby disclaims any responsibility for them.

Any people depicted in stock imagery provided by Getty Images are models,
and such images are being used for illustrative purposes only.
Certain stock imagery © Getty Images.

ISBN: 978-1-9736-8877-8 (sc)
ISBN: 978-1-9736-8878-5 (e)

Library of Congress Control Number: 2020905644

Print information available on the last page.

WestBow Press rev. date: 4/24/2020

This book is dedicated to P.J. Elkins

Special thanks to P.J. Elkins, who first expressed a hope and vision for this book. As a widow, P.J. has faithfully encouraged women and children in Latvia for many years. Special thanks as well to all of the people who saw the value of this project. They have supported P.J. and others like her in their desire to help the hurting and point them to true Hope.

The Author

Jeff Davenport is an author and speaker who encourages audiences of all ages. He and his wife Beth live in West Virginia and have three adult children and four grandchildren.

The Illustrator

Scott Glenn Elkins is a freelance artist and the son of P.J. Elkins, for whom this book is dedicated. He and his wife Nora live in Orlando, Florida and have four adult children and four grandchildren.

There are lots of nice people who care about others.
They might be your teacher or father or mother.

Nice people are kind with
smiles on their faces!
They give you high-fives
and tie your shoelaces.

Nice people are shaped in all kinds of sizes.
Some are short gals and others tall guys-es.

Some have brown eyes
and others big warts.
Some wear nice suits and
others wear shorts.

You can't always tell by
the way that they look,
Just like with the cover, you
can't judge the book.

But sadly, there're people who aren't very nice.
So, here's some important safety advice.
They might be a man, a kid, or a lady.
Let's give them a name; we'll
just call them SHADY.

When something is SHADY
it's not dark or light.
It's so hard to tell if it's
wrong or it's right.

A SHADY person may
seem to be kind,
But really, they're mean
and sick in their mind.

SHADY could even be someone you know,
A neighbor, your family, or an average Joe.
A SHADY could be a friend that you've had,
Who turns into Shady and does something bad.

So, if you feel nervous with how someone's acting,
Be sure to tell others; you're not over-reacting.
You're making yourself a smart safety-zone,
Cause you don't feel safe with SHADY alone.

Cause a SHADY will try to get you to do,
Things that should never be asked of you.
Like a secret touch in your most private place.
Or to see naked pictures with
a smile on their face.

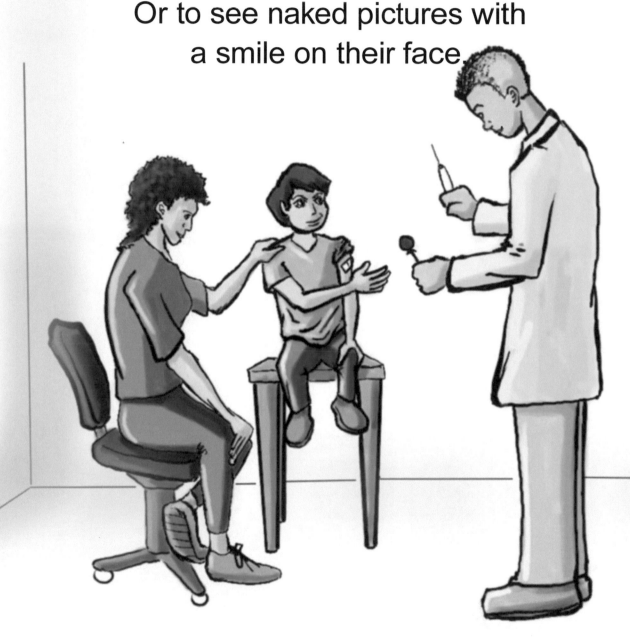

There are private parts only Mommy should see.
Or your doctor or nurse if Mommy's with me.
No one should ask you what's under your clothes,
Those things are private; you decide who knows.

When you feel like SHADY is getting too close,
Or think to yourself, "Now, that is just gross!"
You might even feel mixed-up in your head,
With something that Shady has done or said.

We all have alarms built into our heart,
They help us to know when to stop or to start.
So, if it goes off and you feel you're unsafe,
Trust how you feel and find a safe place.

Shady may say, "don't tell anyone;
If others find out they'll spoil our fun."
Shady is wrong! This must be said,
Body Secrets should never just stay in your head.

If you can't find a friend or
someone you know.
Go find an adult, just get up and go!
The person you tell may seem all upset,
They're not mad at you, so
please do not fret.

But what if I tell and no one believes?
Or if they get mad and somebody leaves?
Remember the truth should always be told.
The truth makes you safe, so speak out, be bold!

If you tell on SHADY you won't be in trouble,
So, if somethings happened go tell on the double.
You're not to blame, you did nothing wrong,
Go tell an adult, and don't wait too long.

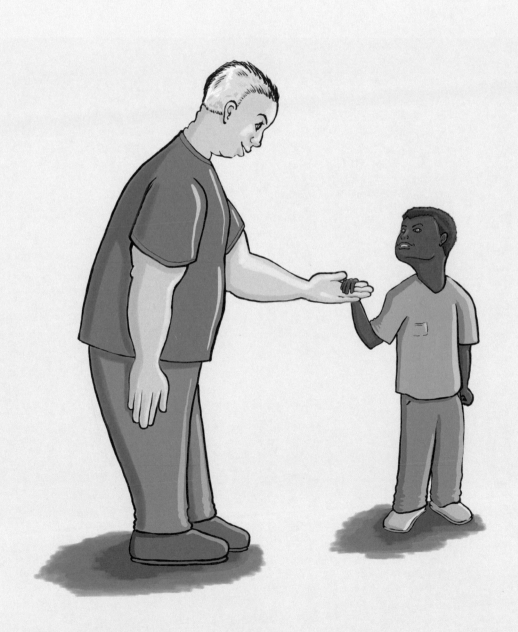

There are a few SHADY's;
We know they're out there.
But lots more nice people
who really do care.

And now that you know
just what you should do,
Go and have fun and
enjoy being you!

You don't have to fear all the people you meet.
You can smile politely and be kind and sweet.

And it's okay to tell even things that seem gross.
Cause we will protect you and love you the most!

THE END

EXTRA HELP for parents…
10 Things Every Child Should
Know About Body Safety

1. Talk about body parts early.
Name body parts and talk about them early – very early. Use proper names for body parts – or at least teach your children what the actual words are for their body parts. If children need to make a disclosure of abuse this can help make their story more understandable.

2. Teach them what body parts are private.
Tell your children that their private parts are called private because their private parts are not for everyone to see. Explain that Mommy and Daddy (or whoever their trusted caregiver is) can see them naked, but people outside of the home should only see them with their clothes on. Explain how their doctor can see them without their clothes because Mommy and Daddy are there with them and the doctor is checking their body.

3. Teach your children about body boundaries.
Tell your children matter-of-factly that no one should touch their private parts and that no one should ask them to touch somebody else's private parts. Parents will often forget the second part of this sentence. Sexual abuse often begins with the perpetrator asking the child to touch them or someone else.

4. Tell your children that body secrets are not okay.
Most perpetrators will tell children to keep the abuse a secret. This can be done in a friendly way such as, "I love playing with you, but if you tell anyone else what we played they won't let me come over again" or as a threat – "This is our secret. If you tell anyone I will tell them it was your idea and you will get in big trouble!" Tell your children that no matter what anyone tells them, body secrets are not okay. Let your children know that they should always tell you if someone asks them to keep a body secret.

5. Tell your children that no one should take pictures of their private parts or show them pictures of private parts.
This one is often missed by parents. There is a whole sick world out there of pedophiles who love to take and trade pictures of naked children online. This is an epidemic and it puts your children at risk. If you only talk about body safety you might be missing a risk factor. Tell your children that no one should ever take pictures of their private parts. Also, pedophiles like to groom children by showing them pornographic pictures. This is their way of "normalizing" the abusive behavior. Let your children know that no one should be showing them pictures of other people's private parts.

6. Teach your children how to get out of scary or uncomfortable situations.

Some children are uncomfortable with telling people "No" – especially older peers or adults. Help give them excuses to get out of uncomfortable situations. Tell your children that if someone wants to see or touch private parts they can tell them they need to leave to go to the bathroom.

7. Have a code word your children can use when they feel unsafe or want to be picked up.

As children get a little bit older, you can give them a code word that they can use when they are feeling unsafe. This can be used at home, when there are guests in the house or when they are on a playdate or a sleepover.

8. Tell your children they will never be in trouble if they tell you a body secret.

Children often tell admit that they didn't say anything because they thought they would get in trouble too. This is often reiterated by the perpetrator. Tell your children that no matter what happens – when they tell you anything about body safety or body secrets they will NEVER get in trouble.

9. Tell your children that a body touch might tickle or feel good.

Many parents and books talk about "good touch – bad touch" – but usually these touches do not hurt or feel bad. Try and stay away from these phrases, as it can confuse children that are "tickled" in their private parts. A better term might be a "secret touch" – as it is a more accurate depiction of what might happen.

10. Tell your children that even if they know someone or even if it is another child these rules are the same.

This is an important point to discuss with your children. When you ask young children what a "bad guy" looks like they will most likely describe a cartoonish villain. Be sure to mention to your children that no one can touch their private parts. You can say something like, "No one should touch your private parts. Mommy and daddy might touch you when we are cleaning you or if you need cream – but no one else should touch you there. Not friends, not aunts or uncles, not teachers or coaches – no one. Even if you like them or think they are in charge, they should still not touch your private parts."

These discussions cannot absolutely prevent sexual abuse, but children are at a much greater risk without these talks. Knowledge is a powerful deterrent to childhood sexual abuse – especially with young children who are targeted due to their innocence and ignorance in this area. Have these discussions often. One discussion is not enough. This is a topic that should be revisited again and again. Find natural times to reiterate these messages – such as bath time. This can be life-altering information for some families and it has the power to prevent some horrific and traumatic experiences. Please share this resource with those you love and care about and help us spread the message of body safety! [1]

How to Report Child Abuse: Childhelp® is a national organization that provides crisis assistance and other counseling and referral services. The Childhelp National Child Abuse Hotline is staffed 24-hours a day, 7-days a week, with professional crisis counselors who have access to a database of 55,000 emergency, social service, and support resources. All calls are anonymous. Contact them at 1.800.4.A.CHILD (1.800.422.4453).

1   Adapted with permission from, **10 Things Every Child Should Know About Body Safety** (adapted and used by permission from *Natasha Daniels, Child Therapist and Author at the* Anxious Toddler (www.anxioustoddlers.com)

Why is a Children's book about Body Safety needed?

- 1 in 5 girls and 1 in 20 boys is a victim of child sexual abuse;
- Over the course of a lifetime, 28% of U.S. youth ages 14-17 had been sexually victimized;
- Children between the ages of 7-13 are most vulnerable to Child Sexual Assault;
- 60% of sexually abused children are abused by someone in their social circle;
- 23% of reported cases of child sexual abuse are perpetrated by individuals under the age of 18;
- It's been estimated that 14% of sexual offenders commit another sexual offense after five years, 24% after fifteen years. *

Printed in the United States
By Bookmasters